PRAYING
THROUGH THE PANDEMIC

BELOVED, I PRAY IN ALL RESPECTS
YOU MAY PROSPER,
AND BE IN GOOD HEALTH,
EVEN AS YOUR SOUL PROSPERS
3 JOHN 2

BEA DUKES

Praying Through the Pandemic

ISBN: 978-0-9833549-7-0

Printed in the USA.

TABLE OF CONTENTS

INTRODUCTION

Thank you for selecting Praying Through the Pandemic. I was motivated to write this book by a spiritual need for a strategic call to prayer during this unprecedented crisis caused by the novel coronavirus.

According to the Centers for Disease Control and Prevention (CDC)[1], COVID-19 is a disease caused by an infection of the coronavirus known as SARS-CoV-2. According to reports, COVID-19 can vary from person to person. The novel coronavirus, that was identified in China in late 2019, has created a world-wide pandemic and continues to disrupt the global economy, unsettle human lives, and generate daily unprecedented death tolls.

According to worldwide data[2], this highly contagious virus has delivered carnage in over 200 countries and territories globally, with nearly 2 million cases of COVID-19, resulting in over 100,000 deaths. While some areas are suffering more devastation than others, the world has over 3 million COVID-19 cases that have resulted in over 200,000 deaths. Hence, the critical need for an immediate call to prayer. This book provides Biblically based information on opportunities to offer targeted prayers as we pray through the pandemic.

---

[1] Coronavirus Disease 2019 (COVID-19). (2020, March). Retrieved from https://www.cdc.gov/coronavirus/2019-ncov/communication/guidance-list.html?Sort=Date%3A%3Adesc.

[2] COVID-19 Coronavirus Pandemic. (2020, April 10). Retrieved from https://www.worldometers.info/coronavirus/.

PRAYER FOR READERS

Dear Father,

I thank you for placing on my heart and within my spirit the burning need to write these prayers as they were placed upon my heart.

Thank you for your forgiveness, grace, and mercy during these unprecedented times.

I pray that Praying Through the Pandemic will intensively reach the inner spirit of the reader. May your Word flow forth like a river.

May these words ignite the passion to prayer.

May the Holy Spirit descend upon each reader and motivate them to select at least one prayer for this incredible season of our lives.

May you grant an understanding of the need to pray!

May the Holy Spirit demystify the complexity of prayer.

May you receive our simple words as we reach out to communicate with you on our behalf and on the behalf of other, for whom we pray.

May forgiveness abound, may we humble ourselves and pray, may we seek your face, may we turn from our wicked ways, may you hear from heaven and heal our land!

May a revival of prayer break forth in this season!

May the prayers come forth from every person, from every family, from every household, from every place, from every institution, from every church, from every community, from every city, from every state, and from every nation!

May the revival of prayer that begins even now, sustain us now and forever more.

In Jesus Name I pray, Amen

WHY YOU SHOULD READ THIS BOOK

During this worldwide crisis, many of us are called to pray. Often the words to initiate communication with our Heavenly Father escape our lips. Praying Through the Pandemic is provided to beckon the call to prayer. It is my sincere belief that it will ignite a prayer revival within our hearts, minds, and spirits. These simple prayers were scripted to share with you. *Due to urgent need to get these prayers in your hands, I may be brief with this version.*

Chapter 1. Prayer for Medical Personnel on the Front Line

Dear God, in you, I place my faith and confidence, the rock of my salvation!

I come humbly before you today to give you honor, praise, and to glorify your name. I seek your forgiveness and blessing of protection during this incredible pandemic.

In your Word, you promised that you be a shelter in the time of a storm. As the doctors, nurses, therapists, hospital staff, and support workers face each workday, only you know the real dangers that they will encounter.

While they wear physical protective equipment (PPE) for the body, I pray that you grant them divine protection against the invisible coronavirus that causes COVID-19, as well as diseases, and dangers, known and unknown.

I pray dear God that you grant them the strength and stamina to withstand the stresses of their workday.

I pray for supernatural capacity to innovatively use the therapeutic measures and medication in their medical treatment arsenal to combat the effects of this viral enemy.

For the doctors, nurses, and other front-line medical professionals, I pray that they may represent you in every way as they prescribe and administer therapeutic treatments, medicines, and other applicable patient-centered procedures.

I pray for patience and compassion as they interact virtually with families and friends, with repeated calls and inquiries.

For the personnel involved in disinfection, sanitation, and cleaning of the facility and equipment, I pray for their protection against the contagion.

I pray for their personal protective equipment to work its intended purpose, in every way! Keep them dear God, in the shadow of your wing. Help them to hear your voice!

I pray that not even a microscopic droplet of the virus will penetrate the shield of protection that you have placed around any of these who so willingly serve their fellow mankind.

Thank you that are with them when they walk through the deepest, darkest valleys of their work.

Let healing spring forth like a fresh spring. May you be honored and glorified in all that I do and say today.

In Jesus name, I pray. Amen.

SCRIPTURE

"If my people, who are called by my name, will humble themselves and pray, and seek my face and turn from their wicked ways, then I will hear from heaven, and I will forgive their sin and will heal their land." II Chronicles 7:14

CHAPTER 2. PRAYER FOR LAW ENFORCEMENT & FIRST RESPONDERS

Dear God,

I give you honor and praise, for thou art God!

Please forgive my sins and heal our land that has been ravaged by infections of the new coronavirus, SARS-CoV-2.

Today, I lift before you our law enforcement personnel and all first responders, including fire and rescue who put their lives on the line every day to protect us.

Father, you are aware of the dangers associated with their jobs, under normal conditions.

Please give them supernatural protections against the invisible enemy, the coronavirus!

As they selflessly give of themselves to serve their communities, may they dwell in the secret place of the Most High!

I pray that you will bestow a special covering during these unprecedented times.

I lift their mental, physical, spiritual, and emotional well-being before thee.

Replace each fear with a double portion of wisdom and strength sufficiency for each new dispatch!

Guide them as they place their faith, confidence, and trust in you!

Show them your power, your presence and love!

I pray that you will keep them safe from this invisible enemy and from all other harm,

In Jesus Name, I pray, Amen.

SCRIPTURE

"He who dwells in the secret place of the Most High Shall abide under the shadow of the Almighty God." Psalms 91:1

Chapter 3. Prayers for Victims of COVID-19

Dear Heavenly Father,

I come before you this day with thanksgiving, honor, and praise for thou art God!

I pray that you will forgive our sins and heal our land.

I stand in awe and in shock of the magnitude of the devastation of this invisible enemy that plagues our nation and our world!

May you send a miracle upon the land and deliver us from this plague!

Deliver us dear God, from the contagiousness, illness, death, and destruction associated with the novel coronavirus!

Heal us dear God from these afflictions! Deliver all that have been afflicted or impacted by this plague.

I lift them before you one-by-one, household-by-household, community-by-community, state-by-state, and nation-by-nation!

Father, by faith, I know that you can do in a moment what our earthly efforts can never achieve.

Today, I join my fellow prayer warriors as we enter into spiritual warfare against this invisible enemy. We speak your words as we plead the blood of Jesus and bind and loose in Jesus Name!

I plead the blood of Jesus on every person that may breathe or makes contact with this enemy, SARS-CoV-2/COVID-19.

I stand in agreement with my fellow prayer warriors, by faith, this enemy must be cast out!

In the Name of Jesus, I bind every spirit of disease associated with the infectious droplets of SARS-CoV-2/COVID-19!

By faith, I bind the contagion and every symptom and complication associated with this COVID-19!

In the Name of Jesus, I loose healing!

In the Name of Jesus, I loose recovery and restoration upon your people!

Father, we know the prayers of the righteous avail much.

May you hear and receive my prayer today! In Jesus Name, Amen.

SCRIPTURE

"And I will give unto thee the keys of the kingdom of heaven: and whatsoever thou shalt bind on earth shall be bound in heaven: and whatsoever thou shalt loose on earth shall be loosed in heaven." Matthew 16:19

CHAPTER 4. PRAYER FOR VULNERABLE PERSONS

Dear Heavenly Father,

I honor and adore you, our sovereign God.

Thank you for my blessings and for the gift of life.

I pray that you will forgive our sins and heal our land.

I pray for special protection for vulnerable persons who may be more likely to become critically ill from the infectious SARS-CoV-2 and manifestation of COVID-19.

Father, I lift before you the elderly and persons with co-morbidities, including chronic health problems and compromised or weakened immune systems, as well as persons without access to health care, and all people who are considered more susceptible and vulnerable.

Strengthen them where they are weak.

Protect them dear Father, be their hypervigilant shield during this infectious, evil pandemic storm. Protect them from harm.

Give them wisdom to hasten to guidance as you provide for their protection and healing. Grant them resources to mitigate and protect against the matter(s) causing the vulnerability.

Take away their fears.

Fortify their mortal bodies.

Be their comfort.

Be their strong tower.

Give them peace that passes all understanding.

Father let the protective power be upon their forehead and the doorpost.

I pray that the invisible enemy, the coronavirus, passes over them.

For those that may have already have symptoms, I pray that the coronavirus departs from them, and from this place, and shall not come again.

In Jesus Name, we surrender these requests.

Whatsoever we ask in your name, we believe that we shall receive!

May you grant them, according to thy will, Amen.

SCRIPTURE

"And the prayer of faith shall save the sick, and the Lord shall raise him up; and if he has committed sins, they shall be forgiven him." James 5:15 (KJV)

CHAPTER 5. PRAYERS FOR THOSE WHO LOST LOVED ONES

Dear Heavenly Father,

I thank you for every opportunity to communicate with you.

I pray that you will forgive my sins and heal our land from this invisible enemy, SARS-CoV-2/COVID-19.

Thank you for sending your son to die on the cross so that whosoever believes may not perish but will have everlasting life!

We are having trouble processing the escalating death tolls of family and loved ones who become victims of COVID-19 and quickly transition from this life.

I come to you today with a heavy hart asking for strength, compassion, comfort and peace for all who lost loved ones due to this global pandemic.

I pray that you will send an angel to stand beside them when they receive the telephone calls from the hospital or other medical facility.

During this time of lockdown and social distancing, the families and friends are not able to assemble and properly celebrate the life of their departed loved one. Please send your Holy Spirit to comfort them and wipe away their tears.

Overshadow them with your presence as they reflect, privately or virtually, on the life well-lived. Cover them mentally, spiritually, and emotionally with your banner of love, strength, and peace!

We pray dear Father, that you will grant them a special closure during these unprecedented times.

May you hold the families and friends, in your loving arms of protection and peace, during the days, weeks, and months that follow.

According to thy will, Amen.

SCRIPTURE

"Brothers and sisters, we do not want you to be uninformed about those who sleep in death, so that you do not grieve like the rest of mankind, who have no hope. For we believe that Jesus died and rose again, and so we believe that God will bring with Jesus those who have fallen asleep in him.

For the Lord himself will come down from heaven, with a loud command, with the voice of the archangel and with the trumpet call of God, and the dead in Christ will rise first. After that, we who are still alive and are left will be caught up together with them in the clouds to meet the Lord in the air. And so, we will be with the Lord forever. "
1 Thessalonians 4:13-14, 16-17 (NIV)

Chapter 6. Prayer for Our Leaders

Dear Heavenly Father,

I present myself before you on behalf of our community, our state, and our nation.

Thank you for your bountiful blessings, amazing grace, and infallible mercy.

Father, I repent on behalf of our community, our state, and our nation!

I pray that our nation will hear your voice and seek thy face.

I pray that you will heal our land.

I pray for our leaders at every level.

I lift up the executive branch of government, the legislative branch, the judicial branch, state leaders, and community leaders!

I pray that you will guide them in every decision that they make! Grant them strength beyond measure.

Give them a pure heart that withstands the influences of the enemy!

I pray that they have clarity of thought!

Remove any stress, fear, and desire for self-exaltation.

Father, I pray that you surround them with wise counsel that can hear your voice and facilitate the best decisions in the interest of your people.

Speak to them in a voice that they recognize as being you, dear God!

May they accept your words, without fear or trepidation.

May they listen to your commands.

May they decrease in self, so that you may increase in them!

May they turn their ears to wisdom and apply their hearts to understanding.

Give them the capacity to lead courageously, with a heart for your people, during these unprecedented times!

In Jesus name we pray, Amen.

SCRIPTURE

"I urge, then, first of all, that petitions, prayers, intercession and thanksgiving be made for all people, for kings and all those in authority, that we may live peaceful and quiet lives in all godliness and holiness." I Timothy 2:1-2 (NIV)

CHAPTER 7. PRAYER FOR THE MILITARY

Dear Heavenly Father,

Our awesome Father and great God, we are grateful to have the opportunity to have the freedom to worship you freely!

Thank you for sacrificing your Son for the remission of our sins. We stand in the gap today for those in the military and for their families.

I pray for their salvation whether stationed in the United States or abroad and have placed their lives in harm's way for our freedom.

I pray for their protection against this invisible viral enemy and perserverance during the crisis that has completely disrupted the normal operations of our places of employment, our families, our community, our economy, our nation, and our world.

Regardless of where they are serving on a COVID-19 related National Guard, Reserve or Individual Ready Reserve activation or on a regular active duty assignment, we pray that you will keep them safe, alert, and attentive. Help them to focus on the mission at hand!

Please surround them with your presence, strength, and guidance. Help them to hear from you.

Despite this worldwide pandemic, please give them protection from this invisible viral enemy and give them presence of mind, as they have voluntarily sacrificed to serve.

I pray that regardless of what they face, they will be prepared to safely, effectively and efficiently carry out their assigned duties.

I pray that they are led by tactically and technically competent, caring, selfless military leaders.

I pray that those in leadership will boldly lead by example and facilitate the continued development of strong, courageous future military leaders.

For those deployed, please protect their families, comfort those at home, and help them to maintain stability while their uniformed loved one is away serving our country.

May they pray without ceasing and seek to commune with you, their Lord and Savior.

In Jesus Name, we pray, Amen.

SCRIPTURE

"For by You I can run against a troop.
By my God I can leap over a wall."
"God *is* my strength *and* power,
and He makes my way perfect."
"So the Lord lives! Blessed *be* my Rock!
Let God be exalted, The Rock of my salvation!"
2 Samuel 22:30, 33, 47

CHAPTER 8. PRAYER FOR MEDICAL RESEARCH

Dear Heavenly Father,

Praise to Him from whom all blessings of knowledge flows.

Please forgive our sins and heal our land from this invisible enemy, SARS-CoV-2/COVID-19.

Today, I humbly request blessings of supernatural research capabilities for medical scientists and all professionals involved in this unprecedented research endeavor.

We stand in need of miracles and miraculous healing treatments for victims of the coronavirus.

I pray that you will anoint the medical scientists and researchers around the world with innovative skills, scientific capacity, perserverance, stamina, dedication, and passion beyond measure!

May they be surrounded in research and clinical trials with wisdom and spiritual understanding.

We stand in need of therapeutic measures to protect the elderly, children, and people with underlying conditions for whom this virus may have a more detrimental impact.

Grant the medical scientists with compassion for humanity and the supernatural intellectual and scientific capacity to speedily and decisively identify, test, and validate therapeutic measures to protect the people against this invisible enemy, COVID-19.

I pray that medical researchers will speedily find an intervention to quickly mitigate the spread of the novel coronavirus, bring an end to the needless suffering, deliver a halt to the needless loss of lives, and facilitate speedy recoveries and rehabilitations, in Jesus Name.

I pray that with each healing and recovery, that you will receive the honor and glory for all that thy hath done!

In Jesus Name, we pray. Amen.

SCRIPTURE

"Behold, I will do a new thing; now it shall spring forth; shall ye not know it? I will even make a way in the wilderness, and rivers in the desert." Isaiah 43:19

Chapter 9. Prayer During Social Distancing & Quarantine/Lockdown

Dear Heavenly Father,

Thank you for another blessing of life itself.

Please forgive my sins and heal our land of this invisible enemy, SARS-CoV-2/COVID-19.

Father, I know that you recognize that the normalcy that we previously experienced has quickly vanished due to the horrible viral plague.

Grant us emotional resiliency to cope with being shut up in our homes except for essential movement until this plague passes over. Grant special housing blessings for those without homes.

Grant us the mental, spiritual, and emotional capacity to withstand the trauma associated with COVID-19, the sudden changes in our lifestyles, the trauma within our nation and around the world.

Grant favor on all who are impacted by the closing of businesses, loss of income, and loss of normal life itself.

Grant comfort to all who are within their homes and cannot be with their loved ones during this pandemic.

We pray that they can access technology or other methods available that reinforce social distancing and other barriers to prevent spreading the novel coronavirus.

Release the stresses associated with social distancing and other new guidance in place for the protection of mankind from this invisible enemy. We pray that you will fill those voids with the presence of your Holy Spirit!

Father, we pray that you will release the people from anxiety and grant comfort to ease the pressures associated with the impact of the coronavirus!

May your people remain vigilant, watchful, and prayerful! In Jesus Name, I pray, Amen.

SCRIPTURE

"Do not be anxious for anything, but in every situation, by prayer and petition, with thanksgiving, present your requests to God.

And the peace of God, which transcends all understanding, will guard your hearts and minds through Christ Jesus.

Finally, brothers and sisters, whatever is true, whatever is noble, whatever is right, whatever is pure, whatever is lovely, whatever is admirable - if anything is excellent or praiseworthy -think about such things."
Philippians 4:6-8 (NIV)

CHAPTER 10. SHORT PRAYERS

MEDICAL & SUPPORT PROFESSIONALS

Father, bless and provide a strategic umbrella of protection around the doctors, nurses, emergency responders, and all professionals and support personnel on the front lines of this battle against this invisible enemy, the coronavirus. Bless them with adequate protective equipment and empower it to fulfill its intended purpose. Grant them strength, stamina, and patience, as they work in the ground zeros of this devastating pandemic. Amen.

CLEANING/SANITATION STAFF

Father, I lift up the names of every cleaning professional in every hospital, long term care, or medical treatment facility. Since the outbreak of this novel coronavirus, these dedicated workers are now on the front lines against this invisible enemy. Grant them access to the appropriate levels of personal protective equipment and protect them from all harm. Amen.

ESSENTIAL WORKERS

Father, please be with all essential workers who continue to perform public-facing work during this crisis. Bless them with the necessary equipment and resources necessary to protect and disinfect. Protect them from any infection of this invisible enemy that is mutating to and fro seeking whomever it may devour. Amen.

FAITH-BASED LEADERS

Father, I lift up the faith-based leaders who are seeking to comfort the needs of the people during this pandemic. I pray that they can successfully facilitate information sharing and combat misinformation that can be detrimental to the congregation. I pray that their faith remains strong. I pray that the God of all grace and mercy, anoint them with fresh oil that covers and protects them, their families, congregants, and community from an infection of SARS-CoV-2/COVID-19. Amen.

Disproportionally Susceptible People

Father, please place your arms of protection around all persons who are disproportionally susceptible to the carnage of the coronavirus. I know that you do not play favorites and everyone as the same. Create supernatural opportunities for increased awareness, opportunities to learn how to avoid exposure, and grant protection from the novel coronavirus, according to your will in glory, Amen.

Persons Without Employment

Dear Father, I seek a special blessing for everyone that has e lost their income due this devastating coronavirus. I pray that you will bless them with resources to sustain them until this situation is over. Please have compassion on their situation(s). Please grant double portion of strength for their emotional, physical, mental, and spiritual health. May their anxiety be comforted by your love and blessings of resources during this crisis. Amen.

Mental Health Challenges

Father, I seek a special blessing for those with vulnerable minds who may experience mental health challenges associated with the pandemic lockdown orders and guidance. The pressure and strain of being socially isolated can be difficult. May they understand that social distancing does not mean social disengagement or social isolation. May you grant them clarity, emotional peace and mental healing during this difficult season of life. May they feel your presence and the comfort of the Holy Spirit. Amen.

Persons Seeking Essential Items

Father, as I prepare to leave my residential lockdown to obtain essential items, please keep a hand of protection over me. Please allow my protective equipment to perform its designated purpose to keep me from even a microscopic granule from the devastating coronavirus. Please grant me safe travels, grace, and mercy to my destination and a safe return. Order my steps and keep me from all evil. Amen.

Persons Exposed to COVID-19

Father, please help me to cope with the stress of isolation necessitated by exposure to the novel coronavirus. I pray that although I am asymptomatic, I pray that I have not unknowingly passed the novel coronavirus to anyone. If so, I pray that you terminate the existence of all antibodies associated with SARS-CoV-2/COVID-19. I that you grant me the mental, emotional, and spiritual capacity to remain steadfast and endure this isolation period. Amen.

Law Enforcement

Father, bless and protect the police officers, sheriffs, marshals, patrol officers, constables, police chiefs, and all law enforcement officials who selflessly put their lives on the line every day to serve our communities. Even more today, they are now on the front lines of the continued battle against evil and now this new invisible enemy, the novel coronavirus. Grant them presence of mind, knowledge, wisdom, and compassion for mankind. Amen.

LOSS OF LOVED ONE

We pause and bow our heads in sacred silent to honor the life of _____(insert name), who lost their battle with COVID-19, but gained their wings and crown in the gates of heaven. Our prayers bombard heaven for strength and comfort for the bereaved family, as well as the heartbroken friends, colleagues, and loved ones. May you bless and keep them until they meet again, Amen.

CHAPTER 11. SINNER'S PRAYER

SINNER'S PRAYER

Dear God,

I confess to you all of the wrong and sinful things that I have done. I ask you to please forgive me and wash away by sins by the blood that you shed on the cross for me.

I am ready to accept you as my Lord and Savior. Come into my life and make me anew. Create in me a new heart and a right spirit within me.

Thank you God, for saving me and for giving me eternal life with you! I believe that I am now born again, and my sins are forgiven. Live within me for all of eternity.

SCRIPTURE

"If thou shalt confess with thy mouth the Lord Jesus, and shalt believe in thine heart that God hath raised him from the dead, thou shalt be saved." Romans 10:9 (KJV)

CHAPTER 12. SUBMIT A PANDEMIC PRAYER REQUEST

If you wish to share a Pandemic prayer request, please use the following URL:
https://www.surveymonkey.com/r/J7QCMVK.

For your convenience, a Pandemic Prayer request QR code is also provided.

CHAPTER 13. SCRIPTURES TO USE DURING THE PANDEMIC

"All scripture is given by inspiration of God,
and is profitable for doctrine,
for reproof, for correction,
for instruction in righteousness:
that the man of God may be perfect,
thoroughly furnished unto all good works."
2 Timothy 3:16-17

SALVATION SCRIPTURES

"Whosoever calls on the name of the Lord shall be saved."
Romans 10:13 (NKJV)

"For God so loved the world, that he gave his only begotten
Son, that whosoever believeth in him should not perish, but
have everlasting life." John 3:16 (KJV)
Romans 10:13

"But if we walk in the light as He is in the light, we have
fellowship with one another, and the blood of Jesus Christ His
Son cleanses us from all sin." I John 1:7 (NKJV)

"Greater love has no one than this, than to lay down one's life
for his friends." John 15:13 (NKJV)

"For I am not ashamed of the gospel, because it is the power
of God that brings salvation to everyone who believes:"
Romans 1:16 (NIV)

"If you declare with your mouth, "Jesus is Lord," and believe
in your heart that God raised him from the dead, you will be
saved." Romans 10:9 (NIV)

"For by grace you have been saved through faith, and that not
of yourselves; it is the gift of God, not of works, lest anyone
should boast." Ephesians 2:8-9 (NKJV)

PROTECTION SCRIPTURES

"The Lord shall preserve you from all evil;
He shall preserve your soul.
The Lord shall preserve your going out and your coming in.
From this time forth, and even forevermore."
Psalm 121:7-8 (KJV)

"Fear not, for I have redeemed you;
I have called you by your name; You are Mine.
When you pass through the waters, I will be with you;
And through the rivers, they shall not overflow you.
When you walk through the fire, you shall not be burned,
Nor shall the flame scorch you."
Isaiah 43:1-2 (NKJV)

"Though I walk in the midst of trouble,
You will revive me; You will stretch out Your hand
Against the wrath of my enemies,
And Your right hand will save me." Psalm 138:7 (NKJV)

"The Lord watches over you; the Lord is your shade at your
right hand; the sun will not harm you by day, nor the moon
by night. The Lord will keep you from all harm, he will watch
over your life; the Lord will watch over your coming and
going both now and forevermore."
Psalm 121:5-8 (NIV)

"The Lord is thy keeper: the Lord is thy shade upon thy right
hand." Psalm 121:5 (KJV)

HEALING SCRIPTURES

"But he was wounded for our transgressions, he was bruised for our iniquities: the chastisement of our peace was upon him; and with his stripes we are healed." Isaiah 53:5 (KJV)

"I am the Lord that healeth thee." Exodus 15:26 (KJV)

"But if the Spirit of Him who raised Jesus from the dead dwells in you, He who raised Christ from the dead will also give life to your mortal bodies through His Spirit who dwells in you." Romans 8:11 (NKVJ)

"Turn to me and be gracious to me, for I am lonely and afflicted." Psalm 25:16 (NIV)

Jesus looked at them and said, "With man this is impossible, but not with God; all things are possible with God." Mark 10:27 (NIV)

"So you shall serve the Lord your God, and He will bless your bread and your water. And I will take sickness away from the midst of you." Exodus 23:25 (NKJV)

"But I will restore you to health, and heal your wounds,' declares the Lord," Jeremiah 30:17 (NIV)

"Beloved, I pray that you may prosper in all things and be in health, just as your soul prospers." 3 John 1:2 (NKJV)

FAITH SCRIPTURES

"And the prayer of faith will save the sick, and the Lord will raise him up. And if he has committed sins, he will be forgiven." James 5:15 (NKJV)

"So then faith cometh by hearing, and hearing by the word of God." Romans 10:17 (KJV)

'If you have faith as a mustard seed, you will say to this mountain, 'Move from here to there,' and it will move; and nothing will be impossible for you." Matthew 17:20 (NKJV)

"Jesus said to him, "If you can believe, all things are possible to him who believes." Mark 9:23

"Jesus said to him, "Go your way; your son lives." So the man believed the word that Jesus spoke to him, and he went his way." John 4:50

"And He said to her, "Daughter, your faith has made you well. Go in peace and be healed of your affliction."
Mark 5:34 (NKJV)

"..the blind men came to Him. And Jesus said to them, "Do you believe that I am able to do this?" They said to Him, "Yes, Lord." Then He touched their eyes, saying, "According to your faith let it be to you." Mathew 9:28-29 (NKJV)

"For it is by grace you have been saved, through faith, and this is not from yourselves, it is the gift of God, not by works." Ephesians 2:8-10 (NKJV)

COMFORTING SCRIPTURES

"Yea, though I walk through the valley of the shadow of
death, I will fear no evil; For You *are* with me;
Your rod and Your staff, they comfort me." Psalm 23:4 (NKJV)

"Blessed are they that mourn: for they shall be comforted."
Matthew 5:4 (KJV)

"Blessed be the God and Father of our Lord Jesus Christ, the
Father of mercies and God of all comfort, who comforts us in
all our tribulation, that we may be able to comfort those who
are in any trouble, with the comfort with which we ourselves
are comforted by God." 2 Corinthians 1:3-4 (NIV)

"God is our refuge and strength, a very present help in
trouble." Psalm 46;1

"Lord, thou hast been our dwelling place in all generations.
Before the mountains were brought forth, or ever thou hadst
formed the earth and the world, even from everlasting to
everlasting, thou art God." Psalm 90:1-2 (KJV)

"Hear my cry, O God; attend unto my prayer.
From the end of the earth will I cry unto thee,
when my heart is overwhelmed:
lead me to the rock that is higher than I.
For thou hast been a shelter for me,
and a strong tower from the enemy.
I will abide in thy tabernacle forever:
I will trust in the covert of thy wings." Psalm 61:2-4 (NKJV)

Spiritual Warfare Scriptures

"When the enemy comes in like a flood,
The Spirit of the Lord will lift up a standard against him."
Isaiah 59:19 (NKJV)

"This is what the Lord says to you: 'Do not be afraid or discouraged because of this vast army. For the battle is not yours, but God's." 2 Chron. 20:15 (NKJV)

"Finally, my brethren, be strong in the Lord and in the power of His might. Put on the whole armor of God, that you may be able to stand against the wiles of the devil. For we do not wrestle against flesh and blood, but against principalities, against powers, against the rulers of the darkness of this age, against spiritual hosts of wickedness in the heavenly places. Therefore, take up the whole armor of God, that you may be able to withstand in the evil day, and having done all, to stand." Ephesians 6:10-13 (NKJV)

"For though we walk in the flesh, we do not war according to the flesh. For the weapons of our warfare are not carnal but mighty in God for pulling down strongholds, casting down arguments and every high thing that exalts itself against the knowledge of God, bringing every thought into captivity to the obedience of Christ," 2 Corinthians 10:3-5

"What shall we then say to these things? If God be for us, who can be against us?" Romans. 8:31 (KJV)

"In all these things, we are more than conquerors through Him who loved us." Romans 8:37 (NKJV)

GOD'S PROMISE SCRIPTURES

"It is of the Lord's mercies that we are not consumed,
because his compassions fail not.
They are new every morning: great is thy faithfulness."
Lamentations 3:22-23

"I am the good shepherd: the good shepherd giveth his life
for the sheep." John 10:11 (KJV)

"Hear my cry, O God; attend unto my prayer.
From the end of the earth will I cry unto thee,
when my heart is overwhelmed:
lead me to the rock that is higher than I.
For thou hast been a shelter for me,
and a strong tower from the enemy.
I will abide in thy tabernacle for ever:
I will trust in the covert of thy wings."
Psalm 61:2-4 (KJV)

"Behold, I will do a new thing; now it shall spring forth; shall
ye not know it? I will even make a way in the wilderness, and
rivers in the desert."
Isaiah 43:19 (KJV)

"Wherefore seeing we also are compassed about with so
great a cloud of witnesses, let us lay aside every weight, and
the sin which doth so easily beset us, and let us run with
patience the race that is set before us."
Hebrews 12:1 (NJKV)

BEREAVEMENT SCRIPTURES

"And I heard a voice from heaven saying unto me, Write, Blessed are the dead which die in the Lord from henceforth: Yea, saith the Spirit, that they may rest from their labours; and their works do follow them." Revelations 14:13 (KJV)

"And God shall wipe away all tears from their eyes; and there shall be no more death, neither sorrow, nor crying, neither shall there be any more pain: for the former things are passed away." Revelation 21:4 (KJV)

"But I do not want you to be ignorant, brethren, concerning those who have fallen asleep, lest you sorrow as others who have no hope. For if we believe that Jesus died and rose again, even so God will bring with Him those who sleep in Jesus." 1 Thessalonians 4:13-15 (NKJV)

"To every thing there is a season, and a time to every purpose under the heaven: A time to be born, and a time to die; a time to plant, and a time to pluck up that which is planted." Ecclesiastes 3:1-2 (KJV)

"I have fought the good fight, I have finished the race, I have kept the faith. Finally, there is laid up for me the crown of righteousness, which the Lord, the righteous Judge, will give to me on that Day, and not to me only but also to all who have loved His appearing." 2 Timothy 4:7-8 (NKJV)

"For I know *that* my Redeemer lives,
And He shall stand at last on the earth;
And after my skin is destroyed, this *I know*,
That in my flesh I shall see God." Job 19:25-26 (NKJV)

Works Cited

The scripture references were quoted from the Holy Bible.

Citations from the King James Version are accompanied with (KJF).

Citations from The New King James Version are accompanied with (NKJV).

Citations from the New International Version are accompanied with (NIV).

Bibliography

Holy Bible: The King James Version.

Holy Bible: The New King James Version. (1982). Nashville: Thomas Nelson.

The Holy Bible, new international version. (1984). Grand Rapids: Zondervan Publishing House.

Coronavirus Disease 2019 (COVID-19). (2020, March). Retrieved from https://www.cdc.gov/coronavirus/2019-ncov/communication/guidance-list.html?Sort=Date%3A%3Adesc.

COVID-19 Coronavirus Pandemic. (2020, April 9). Retrieved from https://www.worldometers.info/coronavirus/

AUTHOR COMMENTARY

I am a prayer warrior, who believes that mustard seed faith can move mountains, and that the prayers of the righteous avail much. As a Mom, wife, military veteran, volunteer, working professional, student, life-long learner, and volunteer, I am committed to a life of servant leadership.

My faith-based resume includes ministry leader, conference speaker, workshop facilitator, panel speaker, women's ministry leader and participant, youth group leader, motivational speaker, as well as other opportunities where I have been called upon to serve. Although none of us are perfect, having a relationship with Christ is vital to the closure of gaps in our spiritual competence, growth, and development.

Our prayers are a phenomenal way to communicate with our Father in heaven. Prayers equip us with an opportunity to make intercession for our families, for colleagues, leaders, and others. Prayer changes things!

Given the unprecedented pandemic crisis within our nation and around the world, I believe that Praying Through the Pandemic will help to ignite a prayer revival, and a strategic call to prayer, at all levels.

Please pray continuously for those impacted by this pandemic caused by the coronavirus. I encourage everyone to pray especially for those on the frontline of the battle against this invisible enemy!

PRAYER OF THANKS

Dear God,

Thank you for the prayer warriors that have read Praying Through the Pandemic.

Thank you, God, for trusting me with these spirit-guided words. Thank you for the stamina to work the late nights to bring this work to your people.

I pray that you will hear the prayers of every person who uses these prayers.

Thank you, Father, for the blessing of family and friends and for all of those that you have sent into my life.

Thank you for those who stood beside me, when no one else was there.

Thank you in advance for the doors that will open so that others may hear your Word and will surrender their lives to you.

I praise you in advance for the revival of prayer that will break forth like a spring of living water!

For all these things, we ask in your Holy Name! Amen

SCRIPTURE

"The Lord watch between me and thee, when we are absent one from another." Genesis 31:49 (KJV)

YOUR FEEDBACK

If you enjoyed Praying Through the Pandemic or found it useful, I would most grateful if you would post a short review on Amazon. Your support really does make a difference. I read all the reviews personally so I can get your feedback and pray for additional opportunities to speak, to pray, to serve, and to lead.

For he will command his angels concerning you, to guard you in all your ways. Psalm 91:11

If you'd like to leave a review then all you need to do is click the review link on this book's page on Amazon. You may also use the following URL:
https://www.amazon.com/review/create-review/?ie=UTF8&channel=glance-detail&asin=B087189SFT

Thanks again for your support!

"Now unto him that is able to keep you from falling,
and to present you faultless
before the presence of his glory with exceeding joy.
To the only wise God our Saviour,
be glory and majesty, dominion and power,
both now and ever.
Amen."
Jude 1:24-25 (NKJV)

www.ingramcontent.com/pod-product-compliance
Lightning Source LLC
Chambersburg PA
CBHW021147020426
42331CB00005B/933